THE GOLDEN YEARS

1963

text: David Sandison, Arthur Davis

design: Paul Kurzeja

SIENA

196

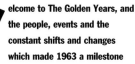

Welcome to The Golden Years, and the people, events and the constant shifts and changes which made 1963 a milestone year for us all. Sadly, the year was dominated by one single terrible event - the assassination in Dallas of John F Kennedy, the young US President who had come to represent a brave new world in which everything was possible, if only we wanted it badly enough and were prepared to work hard to make it happen. The shots which ended his dream would not kill off ours, but the pursuit of them was harder without him, regardless of any human failings he may have had.

Human failings played a key role in the scandal which paralysed Britain for much of 1963 as War Minister John Profumo was shown to be a liar when he told his peers that his relationship with the young Christine Keeler had contained no impropriety. If two-way mirrors, skinny dipping, sex and drug orgies and sharing a mistress with a Soviet naval officer was not improper, someone ought to revise the world's dictionaries. It was highly improper, of course, and Profumo, Keeler and - above all - Dr Stephen Ward would pay a heavy price for their fun and games.

Tragically, fun and games did not feature large in the working life of Dr Martin Luther King, whose fight for

civil rights continued - often with bloody consequences. In August, his leadership of the march on Washington DC would prove a turning point in that struggle as a quarter of a million fellow Americans stood up to be counted.

Earlier that month, a gang of audacious British crooks would be doing their own counting as they shared out the £2.6 million they'd just stolen in what was rightly called The Great Train Robbery. Justice would be swift and merciless for those captured and charged, but Britain did have new folk heroes to grudgingly admire for their cheek and ingenuity.

Despite the tragedies and the losses, it was still a brave, new and exciting world. Let's relive it, one more time!

Labour Loses Gaitskell, Moderate Warrior

BRITAIN'S SOCIALIST MOVEMENT was stunned today by the sudden loss of Hugh Gaitskell (pictured), the 56 year old leader of the Labour Party. He died in hospital after a brief illness which puzzled doctors who'd unsuccessfully attempted to clear a viral infection by using an artificial kidney.

Gaitskell had brought a new philosophical direction to British socialism, but after several years of struggling to overcome the ingrained traditions and prejudices which made the Labour Party unacceptable to the majority of moderate voters, his health finally failed.

Ironically, he had finally succeeded in burying much of the extremism which afflicted the party he took over from Clement Attlee in 1955, but militants within the Labour movement had continually hampered his efforts to make the party electable. His sudden and unexpected death left his party in search of a similarly likeable and patently honest leader to continue the fight to re-establish credibility with an electorate which appeared to have turned its back on socialism.

BBC Relaxes Censorship

That most respectable of organizations, the British Broadcasting Corporation (BBC), relaxed its previously straitlaced standards today by announcing that radio and television comedy programmes would no longer have to avoid or omit mention of so-called 'sensitive' subjects.

The topics which were no longer taboo - including the royal family, religion, leading politicians and sex - were such everyday subjects of debate among ordinary people that a continued ban on their use in humorous broadcasting was seen as government censorship.

The whole area had been brought into sharp focus by the outstanding success of BBC TV's late night satire show *That Was The Week That Was*, whose audience were clearly fascinated by its scriptwriters' determination to break old taboos.

UN Forces Katangan Surrender

The United Nations finally succeeded in enforcing its will on Katanga, the self-proclaimed independent state which broke away from the newly-independent Congo two years ago and had fought a bitter and bloody battle to retain its identity ever since.

Katangan leader Moise Tshombe surrendered today and agreed to submit to the Congolese Government, but requested that he and members of the Katangan government, as well as those who had been under their control - including 200 European mercenaries - should be granted an amnesty from prosecution.

This request was regarded with suspicion by the Congolese Prime Minister, Cyrille Adoula, because Tshombe had broken previous pledges to return Katanga to Congolese control.

However, with a major United Nations presence now in Katanga, Tshombe had no alternative but to agree with Adoula's decision. UN Secretary-General U Thant greeted the news of Katanga's capitulation with relief and obvious pleasure.

UK TOP 10 SINGLES

1: Dance On
- The Shadows

2: Return To Sender
- Elvis Presley

3: The Next Time
- Cliff Richard

4: Bachelor Boy
- Cliff Richard

5: Dance With The Guitar Man
- Duane Eddy

6: Like I Do
- Maureen Evans

7: Sun Arise
- Rolf Harris

8: Lovesick Blues
- Frank Ifield

9: Globetrotter
- The Tornados

10: Diamonds
- Jet Harris and Tony Meehan

Tornados Take 'Telstar' Into Orbit

JANUARY 5

For a British act to reach the top of the US pop charts was an extremely rare occurrence, but The Tornados achieved that when their instrumental hit, *Telstar,* reached No 1 just before Christmas, and proved its success was more than seasonal by staying at the top in this first week of the New Year.

Written by London-based producer Joe Meek to celebrate the launch of *Telstar,* the world's first communications satellite, the hit was recorded at a studio situated in Meek's home in North London, the distinctive acoustics of a tiled bathroom being used to create an echo!

The group was a team assembled mostly from separate groups with whom Meek had worked previously - lead guitarist Alan Caddy had been a member of The Pirates, drummer Clem Cattini had met Meek through The Outlaws, while a vocalist from Glasgow, Heinz Burt, was recruited as bass player. The quintet was completed by organist Roger LaVerne and rhythm guitarist George Bellamy.

The Tornados would remain the only British group to reach No 1 in the US until The Beatles opened the floodgates in early 1964.

De Gaulle Shuts Door On British EEC Membership

THE PERENNIAL DISAGREEMENTS which have afflicted the relationship between Britain and France surfaced again today when French President Charles de Gaulle proclaimed that Britain should not be admitted to the European Common Market (the European Economic Community, or EEC).

According to de Gaulle, the UK could not gain EEC membership while maintaining its current relationship with the countries of the British Commonwealth, or its so-called 'special relationship' with the US, although he hinted that some kind of associate membership might be feasible.

De Gaulle also dismissed the idea of France being equipped with *Polaris* missiles from the US, noting 'We intend to have our own national defences', and suggesting that if the US achieved more prominence in Europe, as appeared to be its ambition, the EEC might soon become of minor importance.

He also accused British Prime Minister Harold Macmillan of attempting to prevent the formation of the EEC in the 1950s by promoting a rival organization, the European Free Trade Association (EFTA).

Britain's chief negotiator in the EEC talks, Edward Heath, said it was unacceptable to break ties with the Commonwealth, while a Foreign Office statement intimated that de Gaulle had been harbouring resentment for some time about ties between Britain and the US.

Soviets Project Nuclear Consequences

Soviet leader Nikita Khrushchev delivered a stark warning to the rest of the world today when he revealed that the USSR now possessed a nuclear weapon of disturbing power - 100 megatons, or ten times bigger than the bombs which devastated the Japanese cities of Hiroshima and Nagasaki in 1945. Khrushchev also chillingly predicted that a nuclear war would result in the deaths of 800 million people. It seemed to many that Khrushchev's climbdown to end the Cuban missile crisis in 1962 had been even more fortunate than was generally supposed at the time.

Frost, JFK's Poet Laureate, Dies

Robert Frost, the closest to a Poet Laureate the US had since President John F Kennedy asked him to read one of his poems at his Inauguration in 1960, died today at the age of 88.

First encouraged to publish his work by the English war poet Rupert Brooke, Frost's poems resounded with the speech patterns, sights and sounds of his native New Hampshire, where he'd begun life as a farmer and cobbler.

Called 'the voice of New England', Frost's first major success was with his collection entitled *North Of Boston*. It was perhaps inevitable that he would be the favourite poet of Kennedy, himself a Bostonian.

FEB

Harold Wilson Is New Labour Party Leader

THE PARLIAMENTARY LABOUR PARTY awarded itself a St Valentine's Day gift today when its members elected Harold Wilson (pictured) as their new leader, succeeding Hugh Gaitskell, whose sudden death in mid-January left many still reeling.

After the elimination of James Callaghan in a preliminary ballot, the parliamentary party was left with a straight choice between Mr Wilson and Gaitskell's deputy, George Brown. After a bruising battle it was Wilson - at 46 years old the youngest ever party leader - who emerged victorious with around 60 per cent of the 247 votes.

'My mandate', said a clearly delighted Wilson, 'is to lead to victory in the coming election, and that is what I intend to do'.

Regarded as a thinking politician - as opposed to Brown, whose tendency to make off-the-cuff proclamations would often be regretted at length afterwards - Wilson announced that he would work to build bridges to allow his vanquished rival to remain as deputy leader of the party, although many felt that two such opposites would be unable to work together without regular disagreements and conflicts.

Journalists Jailed For Contempt In Spy Case

TWO BRITISH JOURNALISTS working for national newspapers were imprisoned for contempt of court in London today after refusing to reveal the sources of information they'd published which had led to the unmasking of former Admiralty clerk William Vassal, convicted of being a Soviet spy last November.

Journalists from the *Daily Mail* and the *Daily Sketch* were given sentences of six and three months respectively. Another *Daily Sketch* writer had received a six months sentence ten days earlier for a similar offence in the same judicial tribunal called to investigate allegations of high-level bungling in the Admiralty.

Lawyers defending the journalists maintained that the decision jeopardized the traditional right of the press to protect its sources of information, but High Court judges ruled that revealing the truth was of paramount importance. The press could not claim immunity from this obligation and possessed no special extenuating rights .

Nkomo Re-Arrested In Rhodesia

Southern Rhodesia's rebel nationalist leader Joshua Nkomo was arrested in the capital, Salisbury, again today - only six weeks after being released from imprisonment - and charged with offences contravening the country's Law & Order Maintenance Act.

Nkomo and four other leading lights of the rebellious Zimbabwe African People's Union (ZAPU) were arrested in the wake of the governmental takeover by the Rhodesian Front. This had taken over from the United Federal Party of Sir Edgar Whitehead, who had banned ZAPU as a terrorist organization four months earlier. The only member of the Rhodesian Front with previous government experience was Ian Smith, who'd been a Parliamentary chief whip. He and his colleagues had made it clear that they would not tolerate black nationalist agitators.

UK TOP 10 SINGLES

1: Diamonds
- Jet Harris and Tony Meehan
2: Wayward Wind
- Frank Ifield
3: Little Town Flirt
- Del Shannon
4: Please Please Me
- The Beatles
5: Globetrotter
- The Tornados
6: Bachelor Boy
- Cliff Richard
7: Loop De Loop
- Frankie Vaughan
8: Don't You Think It's Time
- Mike Berry
9: The Night Has A Thousand Eyes
- Bobby Vee
10: All Alone Am I
- Brenda Lee

ARRIVALS

Born this month:
2: Dan Reed, US pop singer/musician (Dan Reed Network)
9: Travis Tritt, US country music singer, songwriter
19: Seal, UK pop singer, songwriter (*Crazy, Future Love, Killer,* etc)
20: Ian Brown, UK rock musician (Stone Roses)

DEPARTURES

Died this month:
7: Abd-El-Krim, Moroccan statesman, aged 79
22: John Lewis, UK businessman, founder of store chain of same name, aged 68
28: Rajendra Prasad, Indian statesman, first President of the Republic of India

FEBRUARY 9

Seattle - The new Boeing Corporation airliner, the 727, completed its first test flight

FEBRUARY 17

Brandt Back In Berlin Landslide Win

Willy Brandt, the charismatic Mayor of West Berlin, was re-elected to the post today when he enjoyed a landslide win in local elections.

The 50 year old former anti-Nazi resistance fighter, who only returned to his native Germany in 1945 after five years enforced exile in Norway and Sweden, had achieved an international profile via his determined opposition to Soviet and East German threats.

Having risen to the upper ranks of West Germany's Social Democrat Party, Brandt would become its chairman in 1964 and eventually emerge as West German Chancellor in 1969, one of the West's most able and ferocious opponents of Communism, but a man dedicated to reuniting his country.

FEBRUARY 11

Royal Insult For French Leader

A scheduled state visit to France by Princess Margaret, the Queen's sister, was cancelled today.

British Prime Minister Harold Macmillan, who announced the change of plan, said that the cancellation was a direct response to French President Charles de Gaulle's blocking of Britain's application to join the EEC and his ungracious dismissal of President Kennedy's offer of *Polaris* nuclear missiles to equip French submarines.

It was clear to impish commentators that this was a situation in which a Princess kissing a frog would not result in anything positive, although there was now absolutely no likelihood of the French President and the English Princess meeting, let alone kissing...

FEBRUARY 23

Beatles Top The British Charts

A MAJOR NEW FORCE in British popular music emerged today as The Beatles, a quartet from Liverpool, topped most published charts with a song titled *Please Please Me*.

Produced by George Martin, a staff producer for EMI's Parlophone Records previously best known for orchestral albums and comedy LPs by Peter Sellers, The Beatles had been rejected by Decca Records before Martin signed them in 1962 on the strength of some songs they'd written.

The quartet - John Lennon on vocals and rhythm guitar, Paul McCartney on vocals and bass guitar, George Harrison on lead guitar, and the newest member of the band, drummer Richie 'Ringo' Starr - had honed their craft in Hamburg's notorious Reeperbahn, playing for tourists and sailors and backing strippers.

Their love for American country and western, and rhythm & blues music, was reflected in their choice of material, although their first single, *Love Me Do,* which had reached the UK Top 20 in the autumn of 1962, was written by Lennon & McCartney. *Please Please Me* was also the title track of the group's début LP, which was quickly finding a huge teenaged fan following.

Elvis Sticks With RCA

Speculation that Elvis Presley would leave RCA Records this month, when his existing contract with the company expired, proved to be groundless when it was announced that a new deal negotiated by his manager, Colonel Tom Parker, meant that RCA could count on Presley's services until at least 1973 and guaranteed him a minimum of $2 million during that time.

Despite the time Elvis had spent in the US Army between 1958 and 1960, his popularity had apparently remained unaffected by his absence. In the three years since his return to recording and performing, he had released five singles which had topped the US charts: *Stuck On You, It's Now Or Never, Are You Lonesome Tonight, Surrender* and *Good Luck Charm.*

WAR

Cabinet Minister Profumo Denies Dalliance

A BRITISH GOVERNMENT MINISTER, John Profumo (pictured with his wife Valerie Hobson), today told a packed House Of Commons that there was no question of his relationship with a 21 year old model, Christine Keeler, being improper in any way.

Miss Keeler had failed to appear as a witness in a trial at London's Old Bailey, and it had been suggested, under the protection of parliamentary privilege, that her disappearance was somehow linked to Mr Profumo, the Secretary of State for War. The Minister looked pale as he told fellow MPs that he would immediately issue writs for libel and slander if allegations that he was in any way connected with Miss Keeler's absence were repeated in public, adding that he had last seen her in late 1961.

Prime Minister Harold Macmillan later announced that he regarded the issue closed. It had started with rumours linking Miss Keeler - who was also apparently friendly with a Russian diplomat - with an unnamed Minister, inferring that there was a possibility of a breach of national security. This serious allegation did not prevent Mr Profumo and his wife, the actress Valerie Hobson, accompanying the Queen Mother to a race meeting later in the day.

UK TOP 10 SINGLES

1: Summer Holiday
- Cliff Richard

2: Please Please Me
- The Beatles

3: Like I've Never Been Gone
- Billy Fury

4: That's What Love Will Do
- Joe Brown & The Bruvvers

5: The Night Has A Thousand Eyes
- Bobby Vee

6: Foot Tapper
- The Shadows

7: Island Of Dreams
- The Springfields

8: Wayward Wind
- Frank Ifield

9: Charmaine
- The Bachelors

10: One Broken Heart For Sale
- Elvis Presley

MARCH 3

Country Star Patsy Cline Dies In Plane Crash

Fast rising American country & western singer Patsy Cline was killed today in a plane crash, along with two other popular entertainers, 'Hawkshaw' Hawkins and 'Cowboy' Copas. The three singers died with the pilot of their light aircraft near Camden, Tennessee, in an eerie echo of the plane crash which claimed the lives of Buddy Holly, Ritchie Valens and The Big Bopper in February, 1959.

Lloyd 'Cowboy' Copas, who was four months short of his 50th birthday, was enjoying a new lease of popularity after topping the US country charts in 1960 with *Alabam*. The plane was piloted by his son-in-law, Randy Hughes. Harold Franklin 'Hawkshaw' Hawkins would achieve his greatest hit posthumously, when *Lonesome 7-7203* topped the US country chart in May.

But Patsy Cline (real name Virginia Hensley) was regarded as the greatest loss. She had only escaped from a one-sided recording contract which prevented her from achieving her obvious potential not long before the crash.

Tragedy would be compounded on March 8 when Jack Anglin, one half of top country act Johnnie & Jack, was killed in a car crash *en route* to the Cline funeral.

MARCH 16

Death Of Visionary Lord Beveridge

Everyone in Britain who'd ever made use of the country's National Health Service had reason to be grateful to the architect of the British welfare state, Lord William Beveridge, who died today, a few days after his 84th birthday.

The Beveridge Report, published in late 1942, had proposed the introduction of a national system of social security offering support for every-one against sickness, old age and unemployment all paid for by contributions from both employers and workers.

In later years, Beveridge's revolutionary recommendations, which were designed to provide a new national infrastructure when World War II ended, would protect many millions from unnecessary hardship, and help save countless lives.

MARCH 21

Alcatraz, The Escape-Proof Prison, Shuts Down

Inmates of the famous Californian prison, Alcatraz (pictured), were taken to other penal institutions today as the most secure prison in the United States for the past 50 years was closed down.

Sited on an island in San Francisco Bay, Alcatraz was first used as an Army detention centre before World War I, and became a Federal prison in 1934. Its decommissioning was the result of the damage caused to buildings by severe weather - walls built two centuries before had begun to crack and decompose.

Only 27 prisoners were still held in Alcatraz, unlike earlier times when the forbidding stronghold was packed with men their fellow citizens believed too dangerous and violent to be kept in more hospitable and less secure institutions.

MARCH 29

Central African Union Falls Apart

The unsteady political situation in Africa was further destabilized today by the break-up of the Central African Federation (CAF) after the British Government withdrew its support. Active for the past ten years as an attempt to create a unifying grouping, the CAF had opposed increased calls for withdrawal by member nations, and the removal of British backing was regarded by white political leaders of those countries as betrayal.

The British Government Minister for Central African Affairs, Mr RA (Rab) Butler, announced that the newly self-governing Nyasaland, led by Dr Hastings Banda, would be permitted to secede from the CAF, as would Northern Rhodesia. Neighbouring Southern Rhodesia was also expected to seek independence.

SAUSALITO

Beeching Axe Chops British Branch Lines

THE RURAL POPULATION of Britain was in uproar today as British Railways announced the closure of 2,128 stations and the loss of 8,000 rail coaches and 67,700 jobs. The cuts were proposed in a report, 'The Reshaping of British Railways', by Dr Richard Beeching, who'd been 'poached' from the chemical giant ICI by the government, and asked to make the rail network more efficient.

Initial response - from trade unions, the Labour opposition and Conservative MPs in country constituencies listed for Beeching's axe - was unconditionally hostile, and was destined to become even more so as the details, and the implications, became clear.

Dr Beeching, who would need to develop a thick skin as opposition grew, recommended ending all passenger train services north of Inverness, Scotland, and completely closing most branch lines in Central and North Wales, and the West Country. Unless viable alternative bus services were created for those areas, locals could expect to be completely isolated.

Despite a year of protests, strikes, work-to-rule demonstrations, mass pickets and huge petitions, most of Dr Beeching's recommendations would be carried out in 1964, changing the shape of Britain's countryside forever.

Philby, Suspected 'Third Man', Defects

Kim Philby, the British diplomat who in 1955 had survived accusations of being implicated in the 1951 defection of Russian spies Guy Burgess and Donald Maclean, was today confirmed as having vanished from Beirut, where he was working as a correspondent for the *Observer* newspaper, five weeks ago.

Philby - who had been First Secretary at the British Embassy in Washington when Burgess and Maclean disappeared, only hours before the UK-US intelligence net closed on them - had survived a British MP's charge, four years later, that the two had been tipped off by a 'third man'. That had been Philby, who had shared an apartment with Burgess in Washington.

After resigning from the Foreign Office, Philby had worked in Beirut. The arrival, today, of a cable to his wife, who had not seen him for five weeks, ended any lingering doubts. Philby had been the 'third man', and it was increasingly certain he'd joined his former spying partners in Moscow.

BURTON AND TAYLOR IGNORED AS 'TOM JONES' DOMINATES OSCARS

Having established a new record by becoming the most expensive film in history, no-one was over-surprised when *Cleopatra* appeared in the final shortlist for the Best Picture prize in the 1963 Academy Awards ceremony. The money had to be recouped somehow, and new posters mentioning the nomination might help what appeared to be a lost cause.

In fact, the greatest lost cause of all turned out to be that of *Cleopatra's* much-vaunted real-life lovers, Elizabeth Taylor and Richard Burton, who'd started what would become one of the world's most public on-off-on-again relationships while making the movie. Despite their vast fees and a mountain of publicity, neither was even nominated for awards. While co-star Rex Harrison was nominated as Best Actor, *Cleopatra* only managed to retain a shred of credibility with awards for Cinematography, Art Direction and Special Effects.

Surprise hit of the year was the British-made *Tom Jones,* which gathered a remarkable 10 nominations. It won Best Picture Award, another for director Tony Richardson, a Best Adapted Screenplay prize for playwright John Osborne and a Best Score statuette for John Addison.

Leading man Albert Finney and also-nominated co-stars Hugh Griffith, Diane Cilento, Dame Edith Evans and Joyce Redman, didn't get to make the heady walk up, however.

Sidney Poitier made history as the first black American to win the Best Actor award, for *Lillies Of The Field,* while Patricia Neal's brilliant work in *Hud* gave her a well-deserved Best Actress Oscar at the first time of nomination.

The British film industry had more reason to celebrate this year. Both Richard Harris and Rachel Roberts were nominated for their powerful performances in the rugby league drama *This Sporting Life,* while Leslie Caron also came close for her playing in *The L-Shaped Room.* An affectionate cheer was also raised when the gloriously eccentric Margaret Rutherford won the Best Supporting Actress award for *The VIPs,* another Taylor-Burton outing which left many wondering how they justified their inflated sign-on fees.

Hollywood's favourite Italian director, the wonderfully over-the-top Federico Fellini, had lost out in 1961 for *La Dolce Vita.* This year he failed to win the Best Director award for his surreal *81/2,* but was doubtless mollified when it was awarded the Oscar for Best Foreign Film.

Tom Jones

APRIL

Kennedy Honours
British Politicians

In separate events this month, US President John F Kennedy expressed US friendship and appreciation for British politicians of different philosophical hues.

Retired British Tory Prime Minister Sir Winston Churchill, who had co-ordinated and inspired the Allied effort in World War II, was today granted honorary US citizenship by the President in a simple ceremony in Washington. Sir Winston's mother had been a member of a wealthy US family before her marriage, and today's award was long overdue recognition of the especially close relationship the old warrior had enjoyed with US leaders for many years. A few days earlier, Kennedy had also welcomed the new leader of the Labour Party, Harold Wilson, to the White House. It was Wilson's first overseas trip since he took over the reins of British socialism from the late Hugh Gaitskell in February.

Merseybeat Update

With the massive overnight popularity achieved by The Beatles (pictured), a number of other Liverpool-based singers and pop groups were being offered the chance to make records, especially after it became clear that Merseyside was crammed with young performers whose backgrounds and influences were very similar to those of the chart-topping quartet.

Many of the other rising stars from the area were also signed by Beatles producer George Martin and managed by Brian Epstein, a young local businessman who ran the local North End Music Store (NEMS), generally recognized as the best record shop in Liverpool.

Among those already competing for chart success were Gerry & The Pacemakers (whose first single, *How Do You Do It?* went straight to No 1), The Searchers, The Fourmost and Billy J Kramer.

Alabama Governor Wallace Defies Integration Laws

AMERICA'S DEEP SOUTH, where racism had been an accepted way of life since time immemorial, found it hard to come to terms with the newly introduced anti-segregation initiatives of the US government which made racial discrimination illegal.

And few local leaders could compete with the outright defiance of Alabama's governor, George Wallace, who today refused to obey federal orders to enforce integration, even after a visit from US Attorney-General Robert Kennedy, the brother of the US President. After failing to convince Wallace that he was breaking the law, the Attorney-General told reporters, 'It's like a foreign country - there's no communication'.

After a peaceful civil rights protest march in Birmingham, Alabama, was halted by the arrest of its organizers, the Rev Dr Martin Luther King and the Rev Ralph Abernathy - they and over 50 other protesters facing charges of marching without permission - fighting broke out and there were many reported injuries.

However, many of the marchers began singing the anthem which had become the theme tune of the civil rights movement, *We Shall Overcome*, in a gesture of defiance which struck a chord in the minds of many people around the world who watched television coverage of the battle.

Farewell Konrad, Hello Ludwig

Vice-Chancellor Ludwig Erhard, the man who was credited with planning the economic and industrial recovery of West Germany from the ruins of World War II, was today named as the heir apparent of Chancellor Konrad Adenauer when the latter retired later this year.

Adenauer had given his deputy the vital task of reviving Germany's financial fortunes in 1949, an objective the country had to achieve before it hope to regain international credibility after the horrors of the Nazi holocaust. During Adenauer's 14 years as Chancellor, this goal was largely achieved thanks to Erhard's skills.

UK TOP 10 SINGLES

1: How Do You Do It?
- Gerry & The Pacemakers
2: From A Jack To A King
- Ned Miller
3: Foot Tapper
- The Shadows
4: Brown Eyed Handsome Man
- Buddy Holly
5: Rhythm Of The Rain
- The Cascades
6: Say I Won't Be There
- The Springfields
7: Say Wonderful Things
- Ronnie Carroll
8: Summer Holiday
- Cliff Richard
9: The Folk Singer
- Tommy Roe
10: Nobody's Darlin' But Mine
- Frank Ifield

APRIL 25

Government Ministers Cleared In UK Spy Case

NO FRESH SCAPEGOATS emerged from the judicial tribunal held in London to investigate events leading to the prosecution of William Vassall, the Russian spy, which reported its findings today.

The First Lord Of The Admiralty, Lord Carrington, was exonerated of blame for not anticipating that Vassall, a homosexual who worked as a clerk in the Admiralty, was potentially a security risk, while Thomas Galbraith - Lord Carrington's second-in-command - was also cleared of blame in his relationship with the imprisoned traitor.

However, Mr Galbraith had already figuratively 'fallen on his sword' by resigning from his post six months earlier. His departure followed the publication of letters he had sent to Vassall, whom he had innocently, but foolishly, befriended when they worked together at the Admiralty.

It had been the refusal of journalists to reveal the source of those letters, and other confidential documents, which had led to their prison sentences in February. While there were audible sighs of relief in Whitehall's corridors of power at today's tribunal report, anxious glances were beginning to be made towards Moscow, where British businessman Greville Wynne - arrested in Budapest last November shortly after Vassal's conviction - was believed to be on the verge of being charged with spying for Britain.

Police Arrest Mandy Rice-Davies

Although it didn't make headlines, today's arrest of an 18 year old model, Mandy Rice-Davies (pictured), as she was about to leave Britain from Heathrow Airport, would assume major importance in a matter of weeks.

Miss Rice-Davies was the lover of Dr Stephen Ward, a noted society osteopath and gifted amateur artist who counted Prince Philip, the Duke of Edinburgh, among his circle of very influential friends and patients in very high places. It was during a party at Ward's country cottage on Lord Astor's Cliveden estate that War Minister John Profumo first met Christine Keeler, the girl with whom he was now denying he'd had an improper relationship.

The plot was thickening.

70,000 March As CND 20 Arrested

Now a magnet for anti-nuclear groups around the world, the annual London-Aldermaston march organized every Easter weekend by the Campaign for Nuclear Disarmament (CND) began today in Trafalgar Square with a record 70,000 people arriving to begin the two-day, 30-mile walk to the Nuclear Research Establishment at Aldermaston.

The march would gain an extra importance this year as, with the procession nearing Aldermaston on April 17, a spokesman for Britain's Special Branch would announce that 20 CND activists involved in a splinter group 'Spies For Peace' were in custody and would be charged with leaking classified military information to media contacts.

Smuggler Crane Bows In

Female British TV viewers had a new heart-throb interest this month as Associated Redifussion launched *Crane,* a new thriller series set in a seedy Moroccan bar run by its eponymous hero, played by the very rugged and square-jawed Patrick Allen.

Crane was a do-anything, go-anywhere smuggler with a heart of gold and nerves of steel, which he often needed to keep one nimble step ahead of Gerald Flood's elegant police chief. With its apparently exotic location (interiors shot in a British studio, Casablanca courtesy of stock footage) and Allen's undoubted sex-appeal, *Crane* would go on to thrill the ladies for another two years, and result in a spin-off in *Orlando,* a series based on the beachcomber character played by Sam Kydd.

APRIL

Screen Spy 007 Fills Cinemas

FICTIONAL SECRET AGENT James Bond, already an established favourite on the printed page, made a highly successful transition to cinema screens today as *From Russia With Love* opened world-wide, all set to become the biggest feature film hit of the year.

The best-selling books about Bond (who was 'licensed to kill', and often did) were written by former British Naval Intelligence man Ian Fleming, and had already been revealed as President Kennedy's favoured bedtime reading. The part of Bond in both *From Russia With Love* and 1962's *Dr No* was played by Scottish actor Sean Connery (pictured), whose portrayal of the spy as an intriguing mixture of romantic leading man and ruthless assassin captured the imagination of audiences around the world.

Known by the code-name 007 (a 'double O' prefix meant that the agent involved was free to permanently dispose of enemies), Bond was not an overnight screen sensation.

But if *Dr No* had not been an immediate hit with audiences, response to the follow-up was so successful that a third James Bond movie, *Goldfinger,* was already in production while people still formed queues to catch *From Russia With Love.*

Sir Winston Calls It A Day

Sir Winston Churchill, probably the greatest British politician of the twentieth century, finally announced his retirement from the House of Commons today, his resignation to take effect when the current Parliament came to an end.

Aged 88, Sir Winston was in his sixtieth year as a Member of Parliament, and had found it increasingly difficult to move about unaided since he broke his left thigh in June 1962 while holidaying in Monte Carlo.

Sir Winston expressed his regret at the decision to the chairman of the Conservative Association in the Woodford, Essex constituency he had served for many years, noting 'I'm very sad'.

A measure of his frailty was demonstrated when he arrived at a banquet at the Royal Academy this evening and was told in no uncertain terms by his chauffeur and bodyguard that he must use a wheelchair and not attempt to walk from his limousine into the banqueting hall.

Thousands Die In East Pakistan Cyclone

Even by the horrific standards of the region, the tiny, overcrowded and impoverished country of East Pakistan - now Bangladesh - suffered awful devastation today when a cyclone killed an estimated 10,000 people and left at least 500,000 more homeless.

Situated on the delta formed by various large rivers which flow into the Bay of Bengal from the Himalayas, East Pakistan is constantly prey to floods and storms. But today's disaster would stir the international community to launch a massive aid and relief programme as the full extent of the horror became known.

UK TOP 10 SINGLES

1: From Me To You
- The Beatles

2: Scarlett O'Hara
- Jet Harris and Tony Meehan

3: Can't Get Used To Losing You
- Andy Williams

4: How Do You Do It?
- Gerry & The Pacemakers

5: In Dreams
- Roy Orbison

6: Nobody's Darlin' But Mine
- Frank Ifield

7: Do You Want To Know A Secret
- Billy J Kramer & The Dakotas

8: Two Kinds Of Teardrops
- Del Shannon

9: Lucky Lips
- Cliff Richard

10: From A Jack To A King
- Ned Miller

MAY 18

Kennedy Sends US Army To Alabama

Continued and growing racial unrest in the rebellious US state of Alabama had reached the point where President Kennedy felt it necessary to intervene by ordering US Army troops into the state capital, Birmingham, today in an attempt to end the rioting and simmering violence which seemed likely to carry on indefinitely.

The President's move followed the mass arrest of 1,000 blacks taking part in a peaceful anti-segregation protest march in the city. He outraged white supremacists by praising the protesters during a visit to Alabama while his brother, US Attorney-General Robert Kennedy, attempted to broker an agreement between the black and white factions. However, the President's request to black leader Dr Martin Luther King to suspend protest marches until a fresh administration was installed in Birmingham, was rejected. Dr King called Kennedy's initiative 'too little, too late'.

MAY 30

British MP Benn Renounces Peerage

In a move which many less fortunate people could not understand, a special Act of Parliament was approved today, allowing hereditary peers - that is, those who inherited titles - to renounce them and remain 'ordinary' citizens.

This was particularly good news for Lord Stansgate, who, as plain Anthony Wedgwood Benn, had been a prominent Labour Party MP, until forced to stop representing his Bristol South-East constituency when he inherited the title on the death of his father in November 1960. As an earl, he was disqualified from sitting in the House Of Commons.

The new Peerage Bill enabled hereditary peers like him to renounce their titles for life within a month of receiving them, while those who were already peers would have six months in which to make the decision to revert to untitled status. Wedgwood Benn, who had been one of the Bill's major sponsors, was expected to stand for re-election in Bristol as soon as he could, and was also expected to win comfortably.

MAY 16

Gordon Cooper Returns After 22 Orbits

The United States' *Mercury* space programme, the first step in its eventual aim of being first to place a man on the surface of the moon, was the object of admiration and delight today when astronaut Major Gordon Cooper, splashed down safely in the Pacific in his *Mercury* capsule and was picked up by waiting US Navy craft.

Cooper had completed 22 earth orbits during his trip, which made May especially triumphant for NASA scientists. On May 7 they had successfully launched a second *Telstar* communications satellite into space.

MAY 11

No Love In Russia As Wynne Gets Eight Years, Accomplice Gets Death

THE REALITY BEHIND the glamorous world of espionage inhabited by James Bond was highlighted with a vengeance in Moscow today when British businessman Greville Wynne (pictured, left) was sentenced to eight years in prison after being found guilty of conspiring with a Russian GRU (Military Intelligence) Colonel to supply military and political secrets to Western powers.

Wynne was considerably more fortunate than his Russian contact, Colonel Oleg Penkovsky (pictured, right), who was sentenced to death and executed a few days after the four day trial ended. When the death sentence was announced in court, watchers reportedly applauded.

Penkovsky was said to have passed over 5,000 items of secret information relating to Russian military, political and economic policies to the 42 year old Wynne during a period of 16 months, and Wynne had allegedly then passed them on to British and US agents, many of whom were posing as diplomats. Throughout the trial, Wynne - said to have visited Russia and other Eastern countries as an exhibitions stand salesman - protested his complete innocence. After the conclusion of the case, more than a dozen British and US nationals who had been attached to their countries' embassies in Moscow were declared to be no longer welcome in Russia and expelled.

JUNE

Kennedy Wows West Berlin

A crowd of over a million citizens of West Berlin cheered today as US President John F Kennedy addressed them in German to demonstrate his support for them. 'Ich bin ein Berliner' (I am from Berlin) proclaimed Kennedy, and continued, 'All free men, wherever they may live, are citizens of Berlin!'

Accompanied by the Mayor of West Berlin, the former anti-Nazi fighter Willy Brandt, Kennedy toured the divided city in a visit designed to boost the flagging morale of families torn apart by the erection of the Berlin Wall last year.

Kennedy was scathing in his criticism of Communism as he visited the major interchange point for border crossings, Checkpoint Charlie, where signs and banners criticizing West Berlin were displayed on the east side of the border but were also clearly visible from the west.

During the same European trip, President Kennedy was also mobbed by huge crowds as he spent three days in Ireland, taking the opportunity to visit his ancestral home in Waterford on his way back to his present home, the White House.

JUNE 4

Pan Am Orders Concorde

To the intense relief of French and British aero engineers jointly working on building the world's first supersonic passenger plane, to be called *Concorde,* the project received its first major international order today when the US Pan Am airline confirmed its intention to buy the craft.

Sadly, the long-term prospects for *Concorde* would not prove so good. Opposition to supersonic flight over land, problems with landing and take-off noise, and local resistance near airports originally scheduled as destinations, would leave only British Airways and Air France willing to put the aircraft into regular service on a few limited routes.

JUNE 13

Buddhist Monk In Ritual Suicide

The South Vietnamese government's oppression of Buddhists was illuminated in stark detail in Saigon today when a monk named Quang Duc set himself alight in public, suffering an agonizing death as a crowd and TV cameras watched.

The US protested to President Diem about his country's treatment of Buddhists and threatened to censure the predominantly Catholic regime if the oppression continued. A month earlier, South Vietnamese soldiers had killed nine Buddhists during a protest meeting.

The support of the Buddhist population was seen as vital by a US government assisting in the struggle against communist Vietcong forces. Despite President Kennedy's well-publicized Roman Catholicism, he felt obliged to support the Buddhists for what he perceived as the greater good.

Profumo Resigns After Admitting Lies In Sex Scandal

GOVERNMENT MINISTER John Profumo resigned from the Cabinet and the House Of Commons today after admitting that he had lied to his colleagues and Parliament in March when he said that his relationship with 21- year -old Christine Keeler (pictured) had not been improper. He had also maintained that it had not threatened national security, something he also knew not to be true, but the country would soon learn had been. In Keeler, he had shared a lover with Eugene Ivanov, a Soviet naval attaché.

Profumo had been left with no other option after his earlier declaration of innocence had been dubbed dishonest by society osteopath Dr Stephen Ward, whose West End flat had been used for private liaisons by Miss Keeler and the Minister. He had written letters to both the Prime Minister, Harold Macmillan, and Labour leader Harold Wilson, who was quick to attack the Tory leader for the misplaced support he had given Profumo, the Secretary of State for War.

One of the scandal's main victims would be Ward himself, despite - or maybe because - being the one who'd blown the whistle on Keeler's double relationship with Profumo and Ivanov. He would be arrested and charged with living off the immoral earnings of Miss Keeler and the 18- year -old Mandy Rice-Davies. She had been the mistress of slum landlord Peter Rachman before moving in with Ward, and the can of worms she would open under police questioning would cause even wider ripples in the muddy waters already submerging Profumo and the government of Prime Minister Harold Macmillan.

UK TOP 10 SINGLES

1: I Like It
- Gerry & The Pacemakers
2: Do You Want To Know A Secret
- Billy J Kramer & The Dakotas
3: From Me To You
- The Beatles
4: Take These Chains From My Heart
- Ray Charles
5: If You Gotta Make A Fool Of Somebody
- Freddie & The Dreamers
6: Atlantis
- The Shadows
7: When Will You Say I Love You
- Billy Fury
8: Deck Of Cards
- Wink Martindale
9: Scarlett O'Hara
- Jet Harris and Tony Meehan
10: Lucky Lips
- Cliff Richard

Long Live Pope Paul VI

The election of a new Pope has sometimes taken months of deliberation, but the papal conclave of 80 cardinals meeting in the Vatican selected a successor to Pope John XXIII on only the third day of its deliberations. The new Pope, who said he would be known as Paul VI, had been Archbishop of Milan before Pope John promoted him to the rank of Cardinal in 1958. It was widely hoped that the new Pope would continue the attempts at Christian unity which his predecessor had set in motion, starting with the visit of American President, John F Kennedy, whose planned visit to the Vatican had been postponed because of Pope John's illness. Pope Paul VI would be crowned in Rome on June 29.

Bell Saves Clay From Cooper KO

Cassius Clay, the astonishing young US heavyweight boxer universally tipped as world title material sooner rather than later, was saved from a shock defeat by British champ Henry Cooper in London tonight when the bell intervened to rescue both his skin and his unbeaten professional record.

Clay, the ex-Olympic champion from Louisville, Kentucky, had made a practice of accurately predicting - in verse - how many rounds it would take before his opponents would be forced to capitulate. For this fight, he said that it would end in the fifth round, and had opened an old wound over Cooper's notoriously-weak left eye early in the bout. Cooper's left hook in the fourth round, which left a clearly bewildered Clay on his back among the ropes, appeared about to demolish the younger man's record.

Recovered from his upset, Clay waded into Cooper, targeting and re-opening that left eye wound. The referee had to step in, Cooper had lost his chance for immortality, and Clay would live to become the most outstanding heavyweight of all time. *(See Sports pages)*

Russia Launches First Space Woman

A 26 year old Soviet Lieutenant, Valentina Tereshkova (pictured), provided the USSR with another pioneering achievement in the space race today when she became the first woman to orbit the earth.

Russian leader Nikita Khrushchev congratulated Miss Tereshkova, who was said to enjoy parachuting as a hobby, on her achievement. Speaking to her during her epic flight, he promised that her return would be the signal for massive celebration. Another notable aspect of the historical flight was that another manned Russian spacecraft was orbiting nearby, and there was conjecture that the Soviet Union was close to a planned link-up in space.

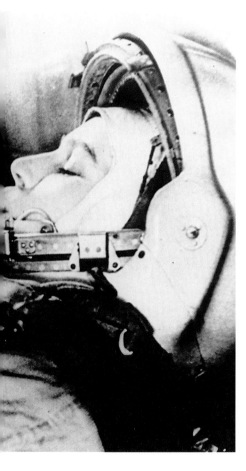

World Mourns John XXIII, The People's Pope

THE LOSS OF HIS FIGHT against cancer today ended the life of Pope John XXIII, who had been a strong advocate of Christian unity and, during his all too brief five-year reign, had become one of the most popular pontiffs in living memory. Certainly, grief at his death was not confined to the world's Roman Catholics, although they were clearly devastated by their loss.

Pope John, who was born Angelo Roncalli, the son of a poor smallhold farmer in a village near Milan, would be remembered for his modern liberal approach to theology and his talent as a diplomat, a vital necessity when reform was the aim.

He had proved his worth as the first post-war papal representative in France, gaining the respect of both extremes of political philosophy and even maintaining a lasting personal and friendly relationship with President de Gaulle, something most world leaders found at least problematic.

Very much a man of the people, Pope John was the first to throw open the Vatican gates and allow outsiders in to look and question. Being interviewed by an American journalist, he was asked how many people actually worked in the Holy City. 'About half!', he replied, grinning hugely.

One of Pope John XXIII's most significant appointments was of the man who was expected to succeed him, Cardinal Giovanni Montini.

JUNE

'ENERY COOPER, THE 'NEARLY' MAN

JUNE 18

British heavyweight champion Henry Cooper, whose scarred face betrayed the fact that he was prone to cuts, seemed on the point of a major upset today when he floored the young American prodigy, Cassius Clay near the end of the fourth round of their non-title fight in London. Clay beat the count, literally saved by the bell, and soon afterwards forced Cooper to retire, unable to see through the river of blood pouring from a cut above his left eye. So near - yet so far...

In many ways that result summed up much of Henry Cooper's career. Undeniably Britain's most popular boxer since World War II, while he enjoyed a remarkably successful domestic career - his defeat of champion Brian London in January 1959 began an unprecedented ten-year reign as British and Empire title-holder during which he saw off eight challengers for the UK crown and became the first man to win three Lonsdale belts outright - he just failed to make it at the very top international level.

Turning pro in 1954 after a distinguished amateur career which included representing Britain in the Helsinki Olympic Games, Cooper had worked his way through the ranks before failing to take Joe Bygraves' Commonwealth title in 1957, and being bested by Sweden's Ingemar Johansson and Joe Erskine to miss out on the European and British titles.

His 1958 wins over Dick Richardson and American Zora Folley had signalled a comeback he confirmed with his 1959 victory over London, but there was no doubt that tonight's loss to Clay was a severe setback. In 1964 Cooper would beat London again to take the European crown, but it would be cuts which ended his 1964 challenge for the re-named Muhammad Ali's world title.

Matched against Jimmy Ellis for the WBA version of the world crown in 1970 after retaining his European title twice (against Karl Mildenberger in 1968) and Piero Tomasoni (in 1970), Cooper resigned his British and Empire title in protest at the British Boxing Board of Control's refusal to recognize the WBA.

His anger at losing the chance to fight Ellis undoubtedly added venom to his attack when he outpointed Jack Bodell later the same year to regain the British title, but the loss - in 1971 - of his British, Commonwealth and European titles to Joe Bugner in a still-disputed points decision, proved the final straw and Cooper quit the game he'd graced for so long.

GREAT DOUBLE FOR NEW BOY NICKLAUS

Only a hooked shot on the last hole of the British Open - held this year at Royal Lytham - stopped newcomer Jack Nicklaus achieving the modern grand slam in only his second season as a professional. As it was, Nicklaus scored the double of the US Masters and the US PGA in a season best described as mixed.

His Masters win at Augusta was achieved in atrocious weather which almost caused the management to halt proceedings on two different days. Nicklaus became the youngest-ever Masters champion at the age of 23, thanks to a second round 66 which put him way ahead of the field, although he had a lucky judgement call at the 72nd hole when his tee shot landed in a puddle left by the torrential rain and he was allowed a free-drop from which he found the green and two-putted to beat Tony Lema by a single stroke.

Nicklaus had a disastrous US Open at Brookline, Massachusetts, failing to make the cut for the last 36 holes, and compounded his misery by hooking on the last hole of the British Open to miss joining Bob Charles and Phil Rodgers in a play-off, which Charles won - the only left-handed golfer ever to win the British Open.

Racing back to the US for the PGA at Dallas Athletic, Nicklaus suffered the agony of yet another last-hole hook. This time he was able to overcome the slip and emerge as winner of Australia's Bruce Crampton, who'd led by three at the three-quarter stage.

RECORDS AND WICKETS TUMBLE FOR FIERY FRED

Yorkshire and England fast bowler Freddie Trueman had a great year, even by his own high standards, as he set a new world Test record for wickets taken during England's winter tour of New Zealand, and then enjoyed a purple patch at Edgbaston in July when his seven for 44 helped England beat the West Indies in the third of the two countries' five-Test series.

It was on March 15, in Christchurch, that 'Fiery Fred' took the five New Zealand wickets (at one point taking three wickets for one run) which took him past Brian Statham's previous record of 242 Test wickets.

Trueman's eventual figures for the match, which completed a 3-0 series win for England, were 7-75 in New Zealand's first innings and 2-16 in their second.

Cooper and Clay - London, June 18th 1963

His bowling in the third Test against the West Indies on July 9 was equally formidable, and enabled Ted Dexter's team to beat the tourists by 217 runs - their only victory in a series which ended with three 'Windies' wins, one England victory and one drawn match.

Trueman's demonic form after lunch that day gave him figures of 6-20 at one stage, and an eventual 7-44, enough to contribute massively to a West Indies collapse and a worst-ever Test total for them of 91 all out. That, and his five first innings wickets, gave Trueman an aggregate for the match of 12-119, a confident answer to critics who suggested that his powers had begun to wane.

JULY 26

Earthquake Shatters Skopje

THE YUGOSLAVIAN CITY OF SKOPJE, which had been razed to the ground during World War II, but had largely been rebuilt to its former glory, was devastated once more today when it was hit by eighty shock waves from an earthquake which left more than 1,000 dead and hundreds of thousands homeless and destitute.

The first shocks were felt around dawn, and were followed by a series of tremors which continued for three hours. An eye witness reported that he was awakened to find his hotel room swaying from side to side.

'I watched the main railway station fall to bits, and as I rushed outside, buildings just collapsed everywhere', he said. 'Screams were coming from under the ruins'.

Refugee camps were established outside the city centre, and emergency supplies, including medical equipment and food, were flown in from the US and Scandinavia. As thousands of people remained trapped or buried under debris, there was concern that epidemics might arise.

There was understandable widespread panic as buildings all over the city centre - identified by geologists as being the earthquake's epicentre - collapsed, including the Town Hall, blocks of offices, hotels and even the main hospital. Inmates and staff jumped from the top floors of the hospital as it began to crumble. Two German tourists were the sole survivors of the 300 guests at a hotel which disintegrated.

The death toll might have been much greater if the earthquake had occurred during the day, when office buildings and shops were full. But that was small consolation for the army of refugees who had survived the carnage but lost everything they owned.

Wilson Denounces Rachman Rent Rip-Off

Christine Keeler, the young woman involved in the case of discredited MP John Profumo and convicted pimp Dr Stephen Ward, was also friendly with the man behind another scandal - London millionaire property developer Peter Rachman. Rachman had operated an iniquitous policy of terrorizing occupants of tenements he owned in London, after which he charged exorbitant rents to unsuspecting tenants for properties which were in many cases no more than slums.

Labour leader Harold Wilson today forced the government to instigate an independent inquiry into rented housing in London when, in a heated House of Commons debate he accused some landlords of being 'creatures of London's underworld growing fat on human misery', and reflected that both the government and the police had taken 'a curiously passive role in this shabby record of gangsterism'.

Communist Superpowers Split

A visit by Chinese communist bosses to the Soviet Union - for discussions about which of their countries could claim to be the world's true keeper of the Marxist flame - ended in deadlock today and exposed the gulf which now existed between the two.

The so called 'peace talks' were the culmination of many months of bitter propaganda exchanges, but the outcome always seemed fraught after Soviet leader Nikita Khrushchev boycotted the meetings. He left Moscow before the Chinese delegation arrived, only returning for a pre-arranged meeting with Britain's Lord Hailsham and US negotiator Averil Harriman on the subject of a nuclear test ban treaty. Any concern that the West had about the two communist giants joining forces and taking over the world was clearly not one which needed addressing immediately.

UK TOP 10 SINGLES

1: Confessin'
- Frank Ifield

2: I Like It
- Gerry & The Pacemakers

3: Atlantis
- The Shadows

4: Devil In Disguise
- Elvis Presley

5: Da Doo Ron Ron
- The Crystals

6: Take These Chains From My Heart
- Ray Charles

7: Sweets For My Sweet
- The Searchers

8: Deck Of Cards
- Wink Martindale

9: Welcome To My World
- Jim Reeves

10: It's My Party
- Lesley Gore

ARRIVALS
Born this month:
31: Norman Cook, UK pop musician, songwriter (The Housemartins), record producer

JULY 1

Philby Confirmed As A Spy

As if it didn't have its hands sufficiently full with the endless embarrassing revelations of the Profumo affair, the British government was faced with a mounting mass of rumour and speculation over the disappearance of erstwhile Foreign Office official Kim Philby in March.

Forced into a corner, the Foreign Office today confirmed that it had been Philby who'd alerted his then colleagues, Guy Burgess and Donald Maclean, that they were under suspicion and should make themselves scarce.

Philby had been accused by MP Marcus Lipton in 1955 of being a double agent, but the allegations were dismissed by Harold Macmillan, then Foreign Secretary but now the Prime Minister. Although he had still not surfaced after vanishing from Beirut, it was widely assumed that Philby had followed Burgess and Maclean to Moscow.

JULY 8

Smith Is First Aussie Woman To Win Wimbledon

Australian men had long dominated world tennis - Sedgman, Hoad and Rosewall most notably - but the first Australian to take the Wimbledon Ladies Singles title was Margaret Smith. Said to play like a man in both style and strength, the 20 year old had been favourite to take the title twice before, but her temperament had unexpectedly let her down and she had not even made the finals.

Today, at the third time of asking, she made no mistake, beating 19 year old American Billie-Jean Moffit in straight sets, 6-3, 6-4.

JULY 3

Britain To Adopt Euro Road Signs

Britain's road to membership of the European Community may have been blocked by France's resolute Charles de Gaulle earlier this year, but the government was determined to start showing willing, and prove that the UK could make an effort.

It was announced today that all existing road signs would be replaced with new, European-styled indicators. There was a lot of sense in this, in any case, as it was possible to find any number of very different signs warning drivers of the same hazard. As an increasing number of British holidaymakers now took their cars into Europe and had to get used to European symbols, the British change-over would clearly be of benefit to them, and to the growing numbers of Europeans driving in Britain.

Stephen Ward Overdoses As He's Found Guilty

DR STEPHEN WARD (pictured), the 50 year old society osteopath and artist at the heart of the Profumo-Ivanov-Keeler scandal which had much of the world enthralled this month, was in a coma tonight, his hospital bed under round-the-clock police surveillance. He had been found in a friend's Chelsea flat - his base during the past seven days of his trial on charges of living off immoral earnings. Ward was perhaps never fully aware that the London court would be declaring him guilty even as doctors tried to clear his bloodstream of the huge amounts of sleeping pills he'd taken after writing the 12 letters found by his bedside.

Despite Ward's protestations that he had never accepted money or gifts for procuring girls for his many rich, influential and now very frightened clients and patients, and his description of much of the evidence as 'a tissue of lies', he must have known the cards were stacked against him.

That evidence meant a packed court every day, and lurid headlines everywhere as a catalogue of sex, drugs and worse was paraded for public view. Two way mirrors, drug and sex orgies, full-time prostitutes and thrill-seeking good-time girls all had their few minutes of the spotlight's glare - and Stephen Ward found himself abandoned by them all.

Stephen Ward never came out of his coma, and would die on August 3, a sad footnote in history.

200,000 Share Martin Luther King's Dream

THE CITY OF WASHINGTON DC came to a halt today as an estimated 200,000 people - young, old, rich, poor, black and white - marched on the US capital to press President Kennedy's administration to speed up legislation to improve America's civil rights. Among the predominantly black marchers were a number of high profile white entertainers, including film stars Judy Garland, Marlon Brando and Burt Lancaster, plus the fast-rising protest singers, Bob Dylan and Joan Baez.

Civil rights leader Dr Martin Luther King urged that the demonstration should remain non-violent, telling the multitude gathered around the Lincoln memorial, 'Let us not seek to satisfy our thirst for freedom by drinking from the cup of hatred and bitterness'. President Kennedy heartened the protesters by telling Dr King and other black leaders that the march had considerably furthered their cause. But the most memorable speech - and the one destined to become the most quoted - came from Dr King, who inspired millions with his oratory.

'I have a dream that one day this nation will rise up and live out the true meaning of its creed: We hold these truths to be self-evident, that all men are created equal', he said. 'I have a dream that the sons of former slaves and the sons of former slave owners will one day sit together at the table of brotherhood'.

Ward Trial – Witnesses Admit Perjury

The London rumour mill went into overdrive again today when two key witnesses against Dr Stephen Ward - prostitutes Ronna Ricardo and Vicky Barrett - had become the subject of fresh police enquiries today after saying that some of their evidence had been deliberately untruthful.

Vicki Barrett was said to have become distraught when told that Ward had committed suicide as the end of his trial approached. One of the letters left by Ward at his bedside had been addressed to her, and when she read his plea that she tell the truth, she admitted lying when she'd told the court she had used Ward's flat to have sex with clients.

Ronna Ricardo had already retracted much of her early evidence in court, and the new enquiries now centred on allegations of perjury and conspiracy in the trial of Christine Keeler's former lover, Aloysius 'Lucky' Gordon. Keeler's non-appearance at that trial had been one of the events which had sparked off the whole Profumo scandal.

Nuclear Test Ban Treaty Gives Peace A Chance

The Kremlin was the venue for today's signing of a three way test ban treaty ending nuclear weapon tests in the atmosphere, under water or in outer space. The signing ceremony was described by British Foreign Secretary Lord Home as 'a great occasion'. However, while it was a significant step forward towards peace, it was not expected to hasten the end of the Cold War, not least because French President Charles de Gaulle refused to commit his country to the treaty, while Russian leader Nikita Khrushchev - although participating in the agreement with the US and Britain - made it clear that the ban did not mean that disarmament would follow. He stressed that East and West supported politically opposite philosophies which would not be brought any closer by the treaty, and it was generally believed that his decision to align himself with the US was spurred by the Soviet Union's recent arguments with China. While the signing of the treaty was clearly significant, US Secretary of State Dean Rusk expressed a note of caution. No-one, he said, could be certain that the event would have any lasting historical significance.

UK TOP 10 SINGLES

1: Sweets For My Sweet
- The Searchers
2: Confessin'
- Frank Ifield
3: Twist And Shout EP
- The Beatles
4: Bad To Me
- Billy J Kramer & The Dakotas
5: Twist And Shout
- Brian Poole & The Tremeloes
6: In Summer
- Billy Fury
7: Devil In Disguise
- Elvis Presley
8: Wipe Out
- The Surfaris
9: I'm Telling You Now
- Freddie & The Dreamers
10: Theme From 'The Legion's Last Patrol'
- Ken Thorne & His Orchestra

Lord Nuffield - The Tycoon Who Gave It All Away

A remarkable man died today after spending the first half of his life creating a fortune, and the second half finding ways of giving his money away to people who could make better use of it. Lord Nuffield (pictured), Britain's most successful car manufacturer, established the Nuffield Foundation to underwrite hundreds of charitable ventures, giving it a kick-start of £10 million ($20m) of ordinary stock in his own Morris Motors empire.

Born William Morris in 1887, he began life as an apprentice cycle mechanic, fell in love with the fast-growing car industry and by the end of World War I headed one of Britain's most successful motor

AUGUST 22

companies, concentrating on making mid-price family saloons.

Made a baronet in 1929, then a peer, he had accumulated a personal fortune of £27 million ($54m) by 1953, when he resigned all his directorships to devote his time to the Foundation.

AUGUST 18

Degree Diploma For Meredith

James Meredith, the first black student ever to attend the University of Mississippi, received his degree diploma today, marking an achievement few believed was possible.

Meredith's enrolment at 'Ole Miss' in September 1962 triggered a riot by hard-line anti-integration whites which left three dead and almost 100 people injured as 750 Federal Marshals ensured the young hero attended the previously segregated college.

Their presence was ordered by President Kennedy after the Governor of Mississippi, Ross Barnett had used state troopers to stop Meredith's first attempt to register for his course.

Millions Stolen In Great Train Robbery

A ROYAL MAIL TRAIN containing over £2.6 million in used banknotes was diverted by a gang of over a dozen armed criminals tonight. They then robbed the train of its valuable cargo by following a well-planned routine.

One of the boldest crimes ever carried out in Britain, the raid quickly dubbed The Great Train Robbery by journalists, relied upon inside information concerning the route the train would take and a precise knowledge of the terrain.

The raid came at a time when the train's usual high security carriages were briefly out of service. Near a quiet country village some 40 miles north west of London, the thieves tampered with a signal to stop the train and simply uncoupled the carriages containing the loot once the driver pulled his engine to a halt.

As the engine and two front coaches resumed their journey, the gang broke into the stationary carriage containing the banknotes, overpowered the guards and threw more than a hundred mailbags over the side of a bridge onto the road below, where other gang members loaded them into a truck. That was driven to a deserted farm, where it was discovered by police five days later.

The whole brilliant exercise, which began at about 3 am, was accomplished in only half an hour. By the time the train driver, who had been injured trying to prevent the heist, was able to raise the alarm, the thieves had vanished.

The hunt was on. The discovery of the gang's hide-out at Leatherslade Farm on August 13 would be followed by the first arrest - of Charlie Wilson - on August 22.

Saigon Regime Under Fresh Attack From Within

The South Vietnamese government in Saigon found itself under renewed attack this month from its own disenchanted citizens, with its controversial treatment of Buddhists at the heart of its self-inflicted problems. On August 21, police arrested 100 monks taking part in a silent demonstration in the centre of the capital, an act which shocked even the most seasoned Vietnam watchers. Reprisal from the populace came on August 25, when thousands of students marched on the Presidential palace, determined to make their displeasure known. Again the focus for heavy-handed police response, the demo ended with 600 students under lock and key.

White House Phone Link With The Kremlin

A direct so-called 'Hot-Line' telephone link between the leaders of the US and the USSR went into operation for the first time today, its inauguration announced simultaneously by the two governments involved.

The line was installed to prevent misunderstandings like those which had occurred during the Cuban missile crisis of 1962. Then, crucial messages between President Kennedy and Mr Khrushchev were delayed, seriously hampering efforts to reach a peaceful conclusion of a situation which could have triggered a nuclear war.

The 'Hot Line' would only be used in a crisis, and messages travelling the 10,000 miles between Moscow and Washington would be transmitted in code. While it was fervently hoped that such a situation like the Cuban crisis would never recur, the existence of the direct link should mean that communication would in future be considerably simpler, quicker, and clearer.

The emergence and outstanding success of The Beatles in Britain was remarkable at the time, especially as the huge management and marketing teams modern pop acts have at their disposal just didn't exist back in 1963. The Beatles became the single biggest thing in pop simply because they were the single most dynamic, fresh and vital thing to have hit a staid and safe pop music scene in years.

Having inched their way cautiously through 1962, experienced their rejection by Decca Records and secured only a tentative deal with EMI's Parlophone label, the moderate success of their début single Love Me Do was perhaps all they could have hoped to achieve.

A look at 1963's highlights should help bring home just how it all came right for the Fab Four:

THE BEATLES -IT ALL STARTED HERE

JANUARY
A short tour of Scottish pubs and clubs was followed by the group's first national TV appearance, on *Thank Your Lucky Stars*, when they performed their newly released single, *Please Please Me*

FEBRUARY
The Beatles begin a UK tour as one of the acts supporting Helen Shapiro
11 - At EMI's Abbey Road Studios, they record 10 tracks for their first LP in just under 10 hours!
23 - *Please Please Me* hits No 1 in the UK charts

MARCH
9 - They begin a UK concert tour as support act for Tommy Roe and Chris Montez

APRIL
21 - The group make their first appearance at the annual *New Musical Express* Pollwinners' Concert at Wembley, playing to 8,000

MAY
4 - *From Me To You* hits No 1 in the UK chart, staying there for seven weeks
11 - Their *Please Please Me* album becomes the UK No 1
18 - They begin a UK tour with Roy Orbison

JUNE
4 - BBC radio broadcast the first of the *Pop Go The Beatles* weekly series featuring the group recorded live in the studio, with appearances by guest artists

AUGUST
3 - The Beatles play their last-ever gig at The Cavern, their Liverpool base in the early days

SEPTEMBER
10 - The Beatles receive the Top Vocal Group award from the Variety Club of Great Britain
14 - With 350,000 advance orders, *She Loves You* becomes an instant UK No 1, eventually selling 1.6 million copies

OCTOBER
4 - The group makes its début on the new TV pop show *Ready Steady Go!*
13 - They star as top-of-the-bill attraction on the top-rated *Sunday Night At The London Palladium* TV show, attracting a record 15 million viewers

NOVEMBER

1 - The Beatles Tour begins, with support acts including Peter Jay & The Jaywalkers, The Brooks Brothers and The Vernon Girls

4 - The group appear on the *Royal Variety Show* before The Queen and The Queen Mother

30 - *She Loves You* returns to No 1 in the UK singles chart and their second album, *With The Beatles,* knocks the *Please Please Me* LP from No 1 in the charts, becoming the first album to sell over a million in Britain

DECEMBER

14 - *I want To Hold Your Hand* becomes UK No 1 two days after release, staying at the top for five weeks and selling 1.5 million in Britain and 15 million worldwide

24 - The first Beatles Christmas Show begins a three-week residency at London's Finsbury Park Astoria. Support bill includes Rolf Harris, Cilla Black, Billy J Kramer & The Dakotas and The Barron Knights

SEPT

Black Children Killed In Alabama Church Bomb Blast

FOUR YOUNG BLACK GIRLS died and more than 20 others sustained serious injuries today when a bomb exploded in the 17th Street Baptist church in Birmingham, Alabama, a rendezvous point for civil rights workers. The Rev JH Cross, who was conducting a service at the time, was blown out of his pulpit by the strength of the blast.

FBI agents were immediately said to be *en route* from Washington to investigate this latest racially-motivated attack in a city which had become something of a battleground in the civil rights conflict.

Alabama State Governor George Wallace, who strongly opposed federal integration laws, ordered state troopers to restore order after black protesters had rained missiles on the local police during a protest against the church killings. Sadly, this only resulted in the death of another black youth and the wounding of three others.

Civil rights leader Dr Martin Luther King said he would go to Birmingham to preach his philosophy of non-violence, and sent a telegram to Governor Wallace effectively blaming him for the continued loss of life and labelling him irresponsible and misguided. Dr King's cable also said, 'The blood of four little children and 13 others critically injured is on your hands'.

American Express Will Do Nicely

The era of plastic money drew inexorably nearer today in Britain with the launch by American Express of its charge card, a facility which would enable bills to be paid on production of a personal card. The service had already been available in the US for five years. Its introduction to Britain was seen as a major step forward both in terms of convenience and security. Ownership of a credit card made it unnecessary to carry large quantities of cash and, because shopkeepers were obliged to ensure that the signature on the card matched that of the purchaser, it was said that fraud could be minimized. In fact, American Express was not the first company to introduce credit cards in the US. It followed Diners Club, whose card had been launched in the early 1950s, and was also available in Britain, although it had not become widely used.

Vietnam Hard-Line Worries Congress

The South Vietnamese President, Ngo Dinh Diem, was given his sternest warning about his regime's treatment of Buddhist leaders today by the US government. Acting on growing criticism in Congress, Washington 'advised' President Diem to sack his brother, Ngo Dinh Nhu, from his post as Vietnam's chief of police.

To make sure the advice was taken seriously, President Kennedy ordered Defence Secretary Robert McNamara and General Maxwell Taylor to fly to Saigon and carry out what was described as 'a full review' of the US contribution to the Vietnam War.

SEPTEMBER 9

Scotland's Clark Is Youngest Ever World Racing Champ

Jim Clark, the 26 year old Formula One racing ace today became the youngest racing driver to win the World Championship when he steered his *Lotus 25* to victory in the Italian Grand Prix at Monza to end a remarkable season. Clark, a farmer's son from the Scottish borders, had won no less than seven of the year's ten Grand Prix events to ensure his place in the history books.

Along the way, Clark became only the first man since Alberto Ascari to win four World Championship races in succession - the Dutch, Belgian, French and British - and took on the top names in US racing in the Indianapolis 500, finishing in a creditable second place.

Jim Clark's title also helped confirm the emergence of British engineer Colin Chapman as his Lotus team won the constructors' world championship.

UK TOP 10 SINGLES

1: She Loves You
- The Beatles
2: It's All In The Game
- Cliff Richard
3: Bad To Me
- Billy J Kramer & The Dakotas
4: I Want To Stay Here
- Steve Lawrence and Eydie Gormé
5: I'll Never Get Over You
- Johnny Kidd & The Pirates
6: I'm Telling You Now
- Freddie & The Dreamers
7: Just Like Eddie
- Heinz
8: You Don't Have To Be A Baby To Cry
- The Caravelles
9: Applejack
- Jet Harris and Tony Meehan
10: Do You Love Me
- Brian Poole & The Tremeloes

ARRIVALS
Born this month:
15: Richard Marx, US rock singer

DEPARTURES
Died this month:
4: Robert Schuman, French statesman, Foreign Secretary 1948-53, EEC visionary, aged 77
19: Sir David Alexander Cecil Low, New Zealand born UK political cartoonist, aged 72

SEPTEMBER 26

Denning Report Points Finger At Macmillan

Lord Denning, the man appointed to investigate the débâcle which resulted in the resignation of Cabinet Minister John Profumo, today set a new cat among the Whitehall pigeons when he published his official report. It proved to be no whitewash, but strongly criticized Prime Minister Harold Macmillan and other government ministers. The impending publication of the Denning Report had excited considerable public interest, to the point that hundreds of people waited in queues outside London book shops to buy copies when the report went on sale shortly after midnight.

Over 150 people had been interviewed by Lord Denning including, it was believed, the man who'd appeared in photographs found in Stephen Ward's collection. He was said to have acted as a completely naked waiter at a dinner party, his identity supposedly protected by the use of a face mask.

The Denning Report exonerated many influential figures from involvement in the scandal, but said that Macmillan and his ministers had not dealt with Profumo's relationship with Christine Keeler properly, even though it had badly affected public confidence in the government.

SEPTEMBER 1

Guy Burgess Dies In Russia

A FLURRY OF RUMOURS emanating from Moscow ended today when Soviet officials confirmed that Guy Burgess, the former Foreign Office official whose disappearance in 1951 with his colleague Donald Maclean sparked a major international manhunt, had died a few days earlier. No more details were given, but it was known that Burgess lived in obscurity, with a small KGB pension his only income.

Burgess, Maclean and Kim Philby - still not confirmed as having arrived in Moscow since his disappearance in March - had been converted to communism while students at Cambridge University in the 1930s. All had risen to important posts in British security, and had played key roles in Russian intelligence-gathering during the late 1940s when the Cold War was at its most bitter.

SEPTEMBER 29

Rolling Stones Open Tour By US Rock Stars

A major tour of Britain by international stars of the pop world began today, the main attraction being The Everly Brothers (pictured), one of the world's most successful acts since their emergence in 1957.

Another big American name on the tour was the flamboyant R&B star Bo Diddley, but many British fans were eager to catch their first glimpse of a new group from London, The Rolling Stones.

Mississippi-born Bo Diddley had become a role model for many British beat groups, among them The Rolling Stones, who in 1964 would use Diddley's characteristic and distinctive rhythm to create their first big hit,

an inspired cover version of Buddy Holly's 1950s song *Not Fade Away*.

Fronted by a former London School Of Economics student, Mick Jagger, The Rolling Stones opened the tour each night, their rawness and their music marking them as a group to watch - and a possible rival to The Beatles.

Supermac Quits – Home Is New PM

AFTER SIX AND A HALF YEARS as British Prime Minister, Harold Macmillan resigned today, the most spectacular casualty of the scandal involving Cabinet Minister John Profumo, a Russian spy and various nubile young women. He would be replaced as the leader of the Conservative party - and therefore Prime Minister - by the Earl of Home on October 18.

Macmillan's shock announcement was made from a hospital bed during the Conservative Party's annual conference, held this year in Blackpool. Weakened by a prostate condition and feeling he'd lost credibility, he'd simply decided to quit.

Lord Home - his surname was pronounced 'Hume' - would have to renounce his peerage to take up the office. Ironically, it was thanks to the efforts of the hard-left socialist Anthony Wedgwood Benn to renounce his title as Lord Stansgate that he could do so.

The new Prime Minister was not a popular choice among some leading Tory figures, and it had been widely presumed that Macmillan's deputy, RA 'Rab' Butler, would be chosen as successor to the man once called 'Supermac'. But Lord Home, who would become known a few days later as Sir Alec Douglas-Home, was the choice of Macmillan and a powerful and influential group of elder statesmen which included Sir Winston Churchill.

Among those who said they would not serve under Sir Alec were Iain Macleod, the leader of the Commons, and Health Minister Enoch Powell. In retrospect, it became clear that one possible reason for Sir Alec's appointment was that no blame had been attached to him in the Denning Report into the Profumo affair.

France Mourns The Loss Of 'Little Sparrow' Edith

The entire French nation united in grief today as it was announced that Edith Piaf - one of its most popular showbiz legends - had died, only a few weeks before her 50th birthday. A true heroine to the French people, she had struggled from a harsh, impoverished childhood to become an international star.

Born Edith Giovanna Gassion in Paris during World War I, she had learned her craft touring with her father's vaudeville company as a child, but began working as a street singer and sometime prostitute when she was 15. Five years later, she was given a steady singing job by a nightclub owner, along with the nickname 'Piaf', Paris slang for a combination of guttersnipe and sparrow.

Piaf's connections with underworld figures meant that she was regarded as less than respectable for many years, but her talent - and particularly her highly emotional vocal style - helped her to achieve fame both as a singer and a film star.

She conducted very public and volatile love affairs with a number of prominent celebrities, including French screen idol Yves Montand and a boxer named Marcel Cerdan, but her heavily-publicized problems with drink and drugs, inevitable ill-health and erratic life style, ensured that memorable songs like the famous *No Regrets (Non, Je Ne Regrette Rien)* and *La Vie En Rose* came from the heart and reached the souls of all who heard her.

UK TOP 10 SINGLES

1: Do You Love Me
- Brian Poole & The Tremeloes
2: Then He Kissed Me
- The Crystals
3: She Loves You
- The Beatles
4: If I Had A Hammer
- Trini Lopez
5: Blue Bayou
- Roy Orbison
6: The First Time
- Adam Faith
7: You'll Never Walk Alone
- Gerry & The Pacemakers
8: Shindig
- The Shadows
9: I (Who Have Nothing)
- Shirley Bassey
10: Applejack
- Jet Harris and Tony Meehan

Soviets Decline Moon-Landing Race

In an unexpected announcement, Soviet leader Nikita Khrushchev made it clear today in Moscow that the USSR would not participate in a race with the US to land a man on the moon. Recent events seemed to suggest that there were matters closer to home needing more urgent attention, not least the growing schism between the Soviet Union and the other major world Communist power, the Republic of China.

Yuri Gagarin and Valentina Tereshkova had become the first man and woman to orbit the earth, but perhaps at a too-high cost to a Soviet economy groaning under the weight of vast arms expenditure.

OCTOBER 31

Beatlemania Sweeps Britain

ANY DOUBTS THAT THE BEATLES - John, Paul, George and Ringo - had replaced Cliff Richard & The Shadows as the most adored British pop idols, were dispelled today by the scenes surrounding their arrival for, and appearance in, a TV show at the London Palladium. Several streets in London's West End were blocked for hours by screaming fans who wanted to see the 'Fab Four' in person.

Earlier in the month, news that they were arriving at London's Heathrow Airport had led to an invasion of thousands of fans. That caused a massive traffic jam around the area which delayed the arrival of Britain's new premier, Sir Alec Douglas-Home!

Next month would see the group receive the firmest confirmation yet of their stardom when they appeared on the bill of the prestigious Royal Variety Performance, one of the acts personally requested for inclusion by the Queen.

Labour Leader Wilson's Brave New World

RECENTLY APPOINTED British Labour leader Harold Wilson today announced at his party's annual conference in Scarborough that he was planning for socialism to reflect 'the white heat of the scientific revolution', although his audience seemed uncertain what he really meant.

Wilson had a wonderful opportunity to use his first conference speech as leader to embarrass the ruling Conservative Party in the wake of the Profumo affair which, if he had but known it, was to be shortly

followed by Prime Minister Harold Macmillan's resignation, and the appointment (by secret conclave and not by his party) of the untried Sir Alec Douglas-Home.

However, what Wilson appeared to be addressing, somewhat obliquely, was the question of trade unions enforcing outdated restrictive practices which might hamper technological progress and make Britain less competitive and efficient in the world market.

Algerians To Nationalize French Property

Algerian President Ben Bella set himself on a potentially explosive collision course with France and his country's large French settler population today when he ordered the nationalization of all land held by Europeans.

Elected to office last year when President Charles de Gaulle granted Algeria independence after a long and bloody war between Arab nationalists

and the so-called *pieds noir* - French nationals who'd opted to live, farm and do business in Algeria, but wanted Algeria to remain part of France.

Ben Bella would find himself under attack from an even more dangerous foe on October 17 when a Moroccan force of 10,000 troops launched a fresh offensive against Algeria in what was already a long-standing border dispute.

Jean Cocteau - True Renaissance Man

The death of Edith Piaf today completely overshadowed the departure of another French giant, the artist, poet, playwright and film director Jean Cocteau, at the age of 64.

A true 'Renaissance man', Cocteau excelled in a number of disciplines. A gifted writer, he turned those talents to creating novels - with the decadent *Les Enfants Terribles* also proving a potent inspiration for one of a number of films he would either write or direct.

Cocteau, very much in the vanguard of the *avant-garde* for many years, also wrote operas, devised ballets, was a gifted artist and a much praised poet.

MARCH 5
PATSY CLINE: A MODERN COUNTRY LEGEND

The aircraft crash which killed fast rising American country & western singer Patsy Cline and two other popular entertainers, 'Hawkshaw' Hawkins and 'Cowboy' Copas, today near Nashville, offers one of popular music's most intriguing 'what-if?' puzzles.

What if Patsy Cline had not been killed? Would she have proved even better, or had she already delivered her best? Would her turbulent personal life have got in the way?

Aged 30 when she died, Patsy left behind a legacy of only 120 recordings, many of them lacklustre performances with producers who treated her talents casually. Freed for only a short while from the contract which led to those recordings, she had briefly been allowed to blossom, emerging as one of those rare performers who could transcend musical categories and captivate all audiences.

The hits she had scored in the last year or so of her troubled life (a saga of a stormy marriage, much-publicized affairs, drink and drug problems) included *Crazy, I Fall To Pieces, She's Got You, Sweet Dreams* and *Walking After Midnight* - all of them still hailed as timeless classics.

JUNE 25
GEORGE MICHAEL: NO SLAVE TO THE SYSTEM

One of the most intriguing legal battles of recent years came in 1995 when the High Court in London was the setting for singer-songwriter George Michael's bid to win a release from his recording contract with the Sony company, claiming its terms made him a virtual slave to the giant multi-national entertainment and electronics group.

The young man born Georgios Kyriacou Panayiotou in the north London suburb of Finchley today, had become one of the world's most successful recording artists during a 13-year career which began in 1981 with the formation of Wham!, arguably Britain's top pop act of the 1980s, with Andrew Ridgeley.

After almost five years of huge international hit singles, Michael began a solo career packed with superlative achievements.

Between 1986 and 1991 he'd scored major hits with *Careless Whisper, A Different Corner, I Knew You Were Waiting (For Me), I Want Your Sex, Father Figure, One More Try, Monkey, Kissing A Fool, Praying For Time, Freedom!* and *Waiting For That Day,* recorded albums which broke all kinds of sales and awards records worldwide, and entered the 1990s as one of the world's richest pop stars.

Wishing to change direction, Michael came into conflict with Sony, who didn't want anything but more of the same. Their reluctance to promote his 1991 *Listen Without Prejudice* Vol 1 album, while he refused to make the standard promotional videos to support the various singles released from it, led to his lawsuit, which eventually went against him.

A compromise deal was hammered out later in 1995, under which the new DreamWorld organization founded by Steven Spielberg and record mogul David Geffen 'bought' Michael's contract from Sony. This would seem to liberate him from what he perceived as a restrictive contract and enable him to pursue his artistic destiny the way he wants to, rather than following the established rules of the game.

NOVEMBER 19

JODIE FOSTER: FROM THE BOTTOM TO THE TOP

It wasn't inevitable that Jodie Foster would become an actress - and arguably the finest of her generation - but the odds were always stacked that way. Born in Los Angeles, raised by a mother who worked as a publicity agent for a film producer, she was given her first job, as a bare-bottomed three year old in a suntan lotion TV advert, and was a veteran of more than 40 other commercials by the age of eight.

Precociously intelligent (she could read by the time she got that first job), Jodie made her acting début in an episode of *Mayberry MD,* a series in which her older brother, Buddy, played a regular role, and soon racked up a number of other appearances in major TV shows, including *The Partridge Family, Gunsmoke, Kung Fu* and - for a short while - her own series, *Paper Moon.*

At the age of 13 Jodie became an unwitting *cause célebre* when she was cast as a child prostitute in Martin Scorsese's powerful *Taxi Driver* (a performance which earned her an Oscar nomination) a furore which she, more interested in graduating with honours from the prestigious Lycée Français in Los Angeles, was commendably able to ignore. After emerging as head of her year at the Lycée, Jodie put her acting career on ice and became a literature student at Yale University.

Dreams of uninterrupted study were demolished in her first year when John Hinckley Jr, a besotted fan, tried to assassinate President Ronald Reagan, claiming he did it to impress Jodie. Overcoming this interruption by refusing to discuss it with journalists, Jodie continued her degree course, graduated with honours, and returned to acting.

A powerful but considerate actress (and always prepared to be a team player), Jodie has justly won two Academy Awards as Best Actress - for her portrayal of the rape victim in *The Accused* and the FBI agent on the trail of a serial killer in *The Silence Of The Lambs.* Her light comedic touch in the big screen version of *Maverick* proved that she was not a one-note player, while her appearance as director of the well-received *Little Man Tate* (about a precociously gifted little boy) suggested that Jodie Foster could emerge as even more of a major Hollywood player in the future.

President Kennedy Assassinated

THE WHOLE WORLD seemed to stop in disbelief today as every television and radio news item and all newspaper front pages were given over to the news that US President John F Kennedy had died, shot in the head, while being driven in an open car through Dallas, Texas, *en route* to a political rally.

The 46- year- old Kennedy was sitting next to his wife, Jackie, in the back seat of the car when several shots rang out as the presidential motorcade passed through the open space of Dealey Plaza. The crowd's cheers turned to screams as the President slumped over, and his wife crawled over the back of the limousine to reach out to a secret service man racing to reach the vehicle. Mrs Kennedy cradled her husband in her arms as the car raced at high speed to the nearby Parkland Hospital, police motorcyclists clearing the way with sirens screaming.

The President was so badly wounded that surgeons could do nothing to save his life and, within half an hour of being hit by the bullets, the United States' 34th President's term of office had been cruelly terminated. Crowds waiting outside the hospital for news were distraught as his death was pronounced, and many broke down in tears.

Texas Governor John Connally, who was riding in the front seat of the President's car, was also wounded, but Vice-President Lyndon Johnson, sitting in a following car, escaped injury.

UK TOP 10 SINGLES

1: She Loves You
- The Beatles
2: You'll Never Walk Alone
- Gerry & The Pacemakers
3: Sugar And Spice
- The Searchers
4: Be My Baby
- The Ronettes
5: I (Who Have Nothing)
- Shirley Bassey
6: Blue Bayou
- Roy Orbison
7: Don't Talk To Him
- Cliff Richard
8: Secret Love
- Kathy Kirby
9: Memphis Tennessee
- Chuck Berry
10: Do You Love Me
- Brian Poole & The Tremeloes

NOVEMBER 1

Vietnam's Diem Ousted In Military Coup

Vietnam's unpopular President Ngo Dinh Diem was reported dead tonight, along with his police chief brother Ngo Dinh Nhu, as elements of the Vietnamese military launched a series of attacks to seize key sites in Saigon and overthrow Diem's regime. While the US government would officially regret the deaths of the brothers, within days it would be announced that Washington had recognized their successors and would continue to offer the new regime full assistance in its war against North Vietnam.

NOVEMBER 22

Johnson Sworn In As New President

Like Nature, the US constitution abhors a vacuum, so it was deemed necessary for Lyndon B Johnson, President Kennedy's deputy, to be sworn in as his successor as soon as possible, to hold the reins of power at least until the next presidential election in November 1964 with the awesome added burden of trying to follow in a dead hero's footsteps.

So it was that the 55- year -old Texan took the oath of office in the presidential jet, *Air Force 1*, before it took off for Washington bearing Jack Kennedy's body, his stunned widow - her clothes still stained with his blood - his clearly stunned successor and his pale-faced wife, Lady Bird Johnson.

After *Air Force 1* touched down at Washington, President Johnson told waiting reporters, 'I will do my best, that is all I can do. I ask for your help, and God's'.

He knew he would need both in the coming days, weeks and months.

53

NOVEMBER 25

World Leaders Help US Mourn At JFK's Funeral

John Kennedy, the three year old son of President John Fitzgerald Kennedy, raised his hand in a military salute as his father's coffin was carried from St Matthew's Cathedral in Washington to the gun carriage waiting to carry it in slow procession to Arlington National Cemetery. A moment later he raised his hand again, this time to wipe a tear from his eye.

With his six year old sister Caroline, young John stood with his mother, his uncles Robert and Edward, and other members of the Kennedy family as the President's burial was conducted with solemn dignity in a city silent except for the tolling of a single bell and the tap of muffled drums.

The carriage which bore the President's body to Arlington was pulled by six grey horses, a soldier leading a riderless horse with boots reversed in the stirrups - the traditional military symbol of a dead warrior. At the graveside, which would later be marked by an eternal flame, pipers of the Black Watch played and a lone bugler sounded *The Last Post.*

Representatives of 93 countries had arrived in the US capital to show the respect they shared for the young President. They included President Charles de Gaulle, Prince Philip (representing the Queen), the leaders of all three British political parties, and many other royal families, national and international leaders, all of whom were present at a reception given by President Johnson this evening in the reception rooms of the State Department.

NOVEMBER 22

Huxley, 'Brave New World' Author, Dies

Naturally overshadowed by tragic and world-shattering events in Dallas today, the death of novelist and iconoclast Aldous Huxley passed almost unnoticed. The English born, but California domiciled, author was 69 years old.

Huxley's most celebrated work was undoubtedly *Brave New World,* a satire which visualized a future with few redeeming features, and stood alongside George Orwell's *1984* as a bleak prediction of the decline of civilization. Another novel, *Antic Hay,* was regarded as almost pornographic, while his mystical essay *The Doors Of Perception* was a disturbing vision written under the influence of the psychedelic drug, mescalin.

In the later 1960s, the very successful US rock group, The Doors, would claim that they'd chosen their name in tribute to the Huxley book.

Millions Witness Shooting Of Lee Harvey Oswald

LEE HARVEY OSWALD (pictured), the man who had achieved international notoriety only two days earlier as 'the man who killed President Kennedy' was himself shot dead in the underground car park of Dallas police headquarters today, his murder witnessed by virtually the entire US nation watching on television to catch a glimpse of the alleged assassin of their beloved President.

Oswald was shot by 52 year old Jack Rubinstein (alias Jack Ruby), the owner of a local striptease club, who emerged from a crowd of journalists and onlookers to fire a number of shots into Oswald's ribs.

Once a US Marine, Oswald had been chairman of a committee which supported Cuban dictator Fidel Castro. He had apparently defected to Russia in 1959, but subsequently returned to the US, bringing his Russian wife with him. Oswald had also been charged with killing a policeman on the day of Kennedy's death, but Jack Ruby prevented him facing trial either for that, or the murder of President Kennedy.

Ruby was said to have told police, 'I did it for Jackie Kennedy', but some of the many conspiracy theories still surrounding the Kennedy assassination suggest that Ruby was part of a combined Mafia-CIA-FBI plot, and had been ordered to eliminate Oswald to ensure his eternal silence.

More than 30 years later, and despite official reports which have concluded that Lee Harvey Oswald did kill John Kennedy and that he acted alone, a mass of apparently contradictory evidence remains to keep the conspiracy theory industry in business, not the least being how on earth a known Mafia-linked gangster could have gained access to such an important suspect in the greatest crime in modern US history.

Jack Ruby would be found guilty of Oswald's murder in March 1964 and sentenced to death, reduced to life after a series of appeals. He would die in January 1967, when a blood clot developed in his lung.

NOV

Tearful Keeler Sentenced To Nine Months

PLEADING GUILTY to charges of conspiring to pervert the course of justice, and also of perjury, Christine Keeler - one of the most notorious figures in the scandal which many felt had forced Prime Minister Harold Macmillan to resign - was sentenced to nine months in prison at London's world-famous Old Bailey today.

Keeler was charged after information came to light at the trial of a Caribbean jazz singer, Aloysius 'Lucky' Gordon, her ex-boyfriend, who had been convicted of assaulting her. During that trial, Keeler had denied that others were present when Gordon attacked her, but it became clear that two other men were hiding in a bedroom - men whose identity Keeler did not want Gordon to discover.

Her defence counsel claimed that Keeler was frightened of Gordon, and alleged that she had been treated by the late Dr Stephen Ward as an Eliza Doolittle to his Henry Higgins, but with additional sexual perversions.

Calling her 'a central figure in a drama which has intrigued the world for the past 12 months', her counsel added that she had invested the money she was paid by a newspaper for her life story in property for herself and her mother. The 21 year old broke down in tears as the judge pronounced sentence.

Mandela Treason Trial Begins

In Pretoria today, the trial began of Nelson Mandela, Walter Sisulu and six other leading members of the outlawed African National Congress (ANC) movement, all accused of treason against South Africa's apartheid regime.

Mandela had suffered arrest and imprisonment before, but the discovery of detailed plans to overthrow the white government during a police search of his home gave the authorities a chance to hit Mandela and the ANC with what they believed would be a crippling blow.

The trial would end in June 1964 with the ANC leaders sentenced to life on Robben Island, the harsh penal colony in the icy waters of Table Bay, Cape Town. It would not be until 1990 that Nelson Mandela - by then the martyred symbol of resistance to an internationally loathed racist system - would finally be granted his liberty, free to lead his people into democracy.

Silver Lining In Kennedy Cloud

John Fitzgerald Kennedy - A Memorial Album became the fastest-selling record in history today, having sold four million copies in the six days since it was released. The LP, which included recordings of several speeches by the assassinated President, sold for only 99 cents. Critics of a nation which would not only tolerate such a crass commercial exploitation of an awful tragedy, but also support it so enthusiastically, had their outrage defused by the fact that all proceeds were to be donated to charity.

UK TOP 10 SINGLES

1: I Want To Hold Your Hand
- The Beatles
2: She Loves You
- The Beatles
3: Secret Love
- Kathy Kirby
4: Glad All Over
- The Dave Clark Five
5: You Were Made For Me
- Freddie & The Dreamers
6: Don't Talk To Him
- Cliff Richard
7: I Only Want To Be With You
- Dusty Springfield
8: Dominique
- The Singing Nun
9: Maria Elena
- Los Indios Tabajaras
10: Twenty Four Hours From Tulsa
- Gene Pitney

DECEMBER 27

TW3 Oversteps The Mark

DESPITE A STATEMENT last month that the BBC's all-powerful Board of Governors had ruled that there would be another 13-week series of the popular but controversial satirical TV series *That Was The Week That Was* in 1964, tonight's edition of the show proved to be its last.

The BBC's explanation for dropping *TW3* (as the show was generally known to its fans and foes) was that there would be a general election in 1964 and, because the show was transmitted live, it would be impossible to ensure that its content was politically balanced or suitably tasteful.

Politicians constantly complained about the lack of respect shown them by *TW3*, a notable recent example being a lampoon by link-man David Frost on the way the new Prime Minister, Sir Alec Douglas-Home, pronounced his name.

Should, he asked, a news bulletin about the PM's health be pronounced 'Lord Hume in bed with flu', or 'Lord Home in bed with Flo'?

BBC Director General Hugh Carleton-Greene had been a supporter of the show, but his approval was not shared by other members of the Board, who claimed to be embarrassed by some of the material included. They were nervous that a monster had been created, with an audience of over 12 million whose Saturday evenings were not complete without a fix of irreverent fun.

DECEMBER 10

Aden Uproar As Grenade Injures Ministers

The South Arabian Federation was under a state of emergency this evening, its border with Yemen sealed and more than 100 Yemenis awaiting deportation, after a grenade was hurled into a group of local ministers and British diplomats at Aden airport.

An Indian woman died in the blast, which injured 39 others, including Sir Kennedy Trevaskis, the British High Commissioner. He and the group were about to fly to London for talks on the colony's independence and the future of Britain's military base.

DECEMBER 12

Kenya Joins Independence Club

The continent of Africa once consisted of countries which were colonies of powerful European nations such as France, Belgium, Spain, Portugal and Britain. However, since British Prime Minister Harold Macmillan's famous 'wind of change' speech to the South African parliament in February, 1960, warning that it's apartheid system was out of step with changing times, more and more African territories had gained their independence.

Today, that 'club' was joined by Kenya, the 34th country to shake off its colonial shackles. Like many other African states, Kenya's independence followed a long and bloody war, and achieved self-determination with a leader who had been imprisoned by his former colonial masters. It was Jomo Kenyatta's Kikuyu tribe which had carried out a brutal war with Britain in the 1950s via its dreaded Mau Mau guerrillas, but it was he who'd recently been elected the prime minister to lead his country into independence.

Kidnappers Release Frank Sinatra Junior

The end of the ordeal endured by Frank Sinatra Jr. (pictured with Frank and Nancy Sinatra), the son of the world-famous singer, came today in Los Angeles when his father paid a kidnap ransom of nearly a quarter of a million dollars to ensure his safe release.

Franklin Wayne Sinatra - his father was Francis Albert Sinatra - was only 19 years old when he was kidnapped, and was already making his mark as a cabaret singer in a style similar to that of his legendary blue-eyed Dad, when the heist occurred.

At the trial of the three kidnappers in March 1964, their defence counsel claimed that the whole thing had been no more than a publicity stunt, to which Frank Sinatra, Sr. retorted, 'This family needs publicity like it needs peritonitis!' The three were convicted and received prison sentences, but Sinatra Jr.'s career lost its impetus.

YOUR 1963 HOROSCOPE

Unlike most Western horoscope systems which group astrological signs into month-long periods based on the influence of 12 constellations, the Chinese believe that those born in the same year of their calendar share common qualities, traits and weaknesses with one of 12 animals - Rat, Ox, Tiger, Rabbit, Dragon, Snake, Horse, Sheep, Monkey, Rooster, Dog or Pig.

They also allocate the general attributes of five natural elements - Earth, Fire, Metal, Water, Wood - and an overall positive or negative aspect to each sign to summarize its qualities.

If you were born between February 5, 1962 and January 24, 1963, you are a Tiger. As this book is devoted to the events of 1963, let's take a look at the sign which governs those born between January 25 that year and February 12, 1964 - The Year of The Rabbit:

THE RABBIT
JANUARY 25, 1963
- FEBRUARY 12, 1964
ELEMENT: METAL ASPECT: (-)

Rabbits are peace-loving creatures who hate anything to do with violence, brutality and war, will avoid physical conflict throughout their lives and are committed pacifists. These traits make them good negotiators and communicators of ideas, always compromising to a conclusion which will satisfy all concerned.

Contrary to what one might think, Rabbits do not lack courage. If all peaceable solutions fail, they will fight bravely for their principles.

Rabbits are wise and intuitive creatures, and often streetwise when it comes to world affairs. They see things coming and are always prepared to handle situations by putting themselves in other people's shoes -

talents which ensure that Rabbits enjoy financial stability and security throughout their lives.

Rabbits possess a natural mothering instinct and are ideally suited to all domestic activities. Home is the center of their universe and everything revolves around making it secure. They have an eye for beauty, are often stylish with good taste and artistic potential, but are better recognized for their appreciation which often leads to Rabbits becoming great collectors.

Sensitivity and artistic appreciation often combine to make Rabbits outstanding musicians.

While some Rabbits are described as cold individuals who dislike physical contact, this coolness is essentially a means of masking their deeply sensitive nature - but that sensitivity can also account for Rabbits' notorious moodiness and a tendency to swing from elation to depression at the drop of a hat.

Method, order and routine are important to the Rabbit's well-being - they need a carefully-planned existence.

This does not mean Rabbits are boring, however. They do appreciate sociability and can be friendly and chatty. They also possess the most cultivated social graces and can always be distinguished by their sense of refinement and cultured views. Physically and intellectually elegant, Rabbits will always stand out in a crowd.

FAMOUS RABBITS

Fidel Castro	**Ali McGraw**
President of Cuba	Actress
John Cleese	**Henry Miller**
Actor, writer	Author (Tropic of Cancer, etc)
David Frost	**Orson Welles**
TV personality/interviewer	Film actor/director/writer